i

Table of Contents

Analysis Background and Objectives

This study analyzes the economy-wide impacts of the American Recovery and Reinvestment Act of 2009 (Recovery Act or ARRA) funding for Smart Grid project deployment in the United States, administered by the U.S. Department of Energy Office of Electricity Delivery and Energy Reliability (DOE OE). The time period of the investments analyzed cover expenditures from August 2009 to March 2012, which encompasses nearly three billion dollars in publicly documented expenditures. The Smart Grid support from the U.S. Department of Energy (DOE) included the Smart Grid Investment Grants (SGIG) and the Smart Grid Demonstration Program (SGDP). These investments under the Recovery Act were intended to serve a dual mission: a primary mission of economic stimulus for the American workforce and the nation's economy as a whole, and a secondary mission of supporting the specific program or Agency mission through the authorizing department, which in this case is the modernization of the United States electricity grid. Both missions are reflected in the ARRA Smart Grid projects, as they have generated economic benefits and are beginning to demonstrate that the deployment of Smart Grid technology is leading to operational, customer, and reliability benefits. These benefits, however, are being realized on different time horizons, and the present analysis follows the economic effects of the immediate spending, and represents a measure of performance towards the primary mission.

Key Findings

ARRA funding and matching support from utilities and the private sector in the SGIG and SGDP programs generated a significant impact on the U.S. economy. As of March 2012, the total invested value of $2.96 billion to support Smart Grid projects generated at least $6.8 billion in total economic output.

Smart Grid deployment positively impacted employment and labor income throughout the economy. Overall, about 47,000 full time equivalent jobs were supported by investments. Among Smart Grid vendors - an ecosystem of manufacturers, information technology and technical services providers - about 12,000 direct jobs were supported, with the remaining jobs being in those companies' respective supply chains and induced by the money spent throughout the broader economy.

Investment in core Smart Grid industries supports high-paying jobs. Industrial sectors that benefit directly include computer systems design, technical and scientific services and consulting, and electrical/wireless equipment and component manufacturing. Industrial sectors that experience indirect and induced benefits include real estate, wholesale trade, financial services, restaurants, and health care. Smart Grid ARRA investments also supported employment in personal service sectors such as health care, financial services, real estate, and food/restaurants through indirect and induced impacts.

The Smart Grid Gross Domestic Product (GDP) multiplier is higher than many forms of government investment. For every $1 million of direct spending, which includes both government ARRA funds and private sector matching, the GDP increased by $2.5 to $2.6 million, depending on the scenario being evaluated, which compares favorably against other potential government investments in general spending or other types of infrastructure.

The inputs for this analysis are based on actual SGIG and SGDP payments to vendors reported in www.Recovery.gov made from August 2009 through March 2012, and the associated matching investments made by the grant recipients in the private sector. Matching investments were assumed to be equal to the Federal payments. By confining this analysis to actual payments to vendors, as reported by grant recipients in a publicly available website, the number of assumptions necessary to perform the analysis is low, and these results can be reproduced or analyzed by others.

The key objective of this study is to understand the flow of funds through the ARRA Smart Grid projects to the community of vendors necessary to accomplish these ambitious projects. Many industrial sectors benefit from Smart Grid investments, and the economic and labor impacts are substantially broader than the first line of organizations and companies receiving the funds.

The analysis uses the IMPLAN model (www.implan.com) to estimate the economy-wide impacts associated with two investment scenarios:

- **All Vendors Scenario**. This scenario reflects federal and matching industry investments ($2.96 billion) made to core Smart Grid vendors and those vendors not considered core to the Smart Grid industries but still associated with grid modernization. These non-core vendors include accounting, legal, freight, and temporary employment services and equipment rental, among others.

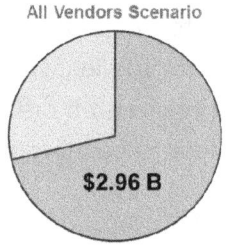

All Vendors Scenario

$2.96 B

- **Smart Grid Vendors Only Scenario**. This scenario is a subset of the All Vendors Scenario, and consists of federal and matching industry investments ($2.11 billion) in core Smart Grid vendors (e.g., systems design, professional services, and electronic component manufacturing), which allows for additional analysis of this important class of companies.

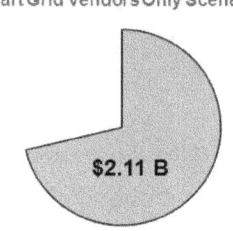

Smart Grid Vendors Only Scenario

$2.11 B

The economic analysis estimates the impact that each scenario has on Gross Domestic Product (GDP), economic output, employment, labor income, and tax impacts. The summary in Table 1 below presents the results for each scenario in terms of employment, total labor income, GDP and economic output impacts. Employment impacts are described in terms of the number of jobs that are supported by the ARRA Smart Grid projects. These jobs may include both newly created jobs as well as existing jobs that would have been lost if not for the investment. Labor income is the value of all forms of employment income, including employee compensation (wages and benefits) and proprietor (owner) income. GDP is the market value of the goods and services produced by labor and property located within the borders of the United States. It is one of the best indicators of a program's impact, as it captures value-added impact, meaning it is equal to its gross output (which consists of sales or receipts and other operating income, commodity taxes, and inventory change) minus its intermediate inputs (which consist of energy, raw materials, semi-finished goods, and services) that are purchased from domestic industries or from foreign sources. In comparison, economic output represents the total value of industry production, or in basic terms, the economic value of each industry's sales. Expenditures from the ARRA Smart Grid program also generate federal, state and local taxes due to the program investment, as shown in the table below.

Table 1 –Summary Results

	Total Impact	
	All Vendors	Smart Grid Vendors Only
Employment (jobs)	47,000	33,000
Labor Income (2010$)	$2.86 Billion	$2.07 Billion
GDP (2010$)	$4.18 Billion	$2.91 Billion
Economic Output (2010$)	$6.83 Billion	$4.79 Billion
State and Local taxes (2010$)	$0.36 Billion	$0.26 Billion
Federal taxes (2010$)	$0.66 Billion	$0.49 Billion

The Smart Grid projects that received funding under these two ARRA Smart Grid programs are representative of typical Smart Grid investment that is expected to occur for years to come in the United States. Follow-on investments, funded by State, ratepayer and private sector sources are likely to have a similarly positive impact profile, and should continue to generate high technology and professional jobs as grid modernization continues. Sustaining and accelerating the pace of electric infrastructure modernization by demonstration, research and information sharing is one of the core missions of the DOE OE.

Introduction

Background

The U.S. Department of Energy's Office of Electricity Delivery and Energy Reliability (DOE OE) is developing a better understanding of the Smart Grid vendor ecosystem and marketplace, and is evaluating the impact of American Recovery and Reinvestment Act of 2009 (ARRA) funds on this marketplace. DOE OE has identified and classified the core Smart Grid vendors, assessed the overall market size and networks of vendors in the Smart Grid domains, and assessed the economic impacts of ARRA investments on these different markets.

Analysis Objectives

The key objective of this study is to understand the flow of funds through the Smart Grid projects and the associated vendor ecosystem that benefit from ARRA Smart Grid funds and to gain a better understanding of the associated economic impacts of the Smart Grid investments on the broader economy.

This study analyzes the economy-wide impacts associated with ARRA funding for Smart Grid project deployment in the United States. The inputs for this analysis are based on actual Smart Grid Investment Grant (SGIG) and Smart Grid Demonstration Program (SGDP) payments to vendors reported in www.Recovery.gov. Payments to vendors for goods and services supplied from August 2009 to March 2012 are included in the analysis. It should be noted that www.Recovery.gov only captures the federal portion of the payments made to vendors, and such payments must be doubled to arrive at the actual amounts to reflect the matching contributions from the grant recipients.

Scope of Analysis

Investments made in the Smart Grid through ARRA are intended to serve a dual mission. The primary mission focuses on the immediate need to provide economic stimulus and job creation. Second, the Recovery Act serves as a mechanism to further support the specific program or agency mission of the authorizing department, in this case, DOE's mission to modernize electricity infrastructure to advance the nation's economic prosperity and security. Both missions are pursued by the ARRA Smart Grid projects, and are expected to generate economic benefit, job creation and labor income. The broader benefits associated with Smart Grid are expected to be realized on different time scales and durations— see Figure 1.

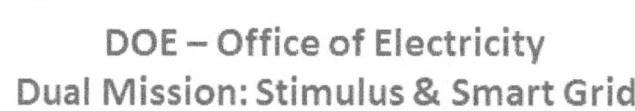

Figure 1 – ARRA Smart Grid Project Mission

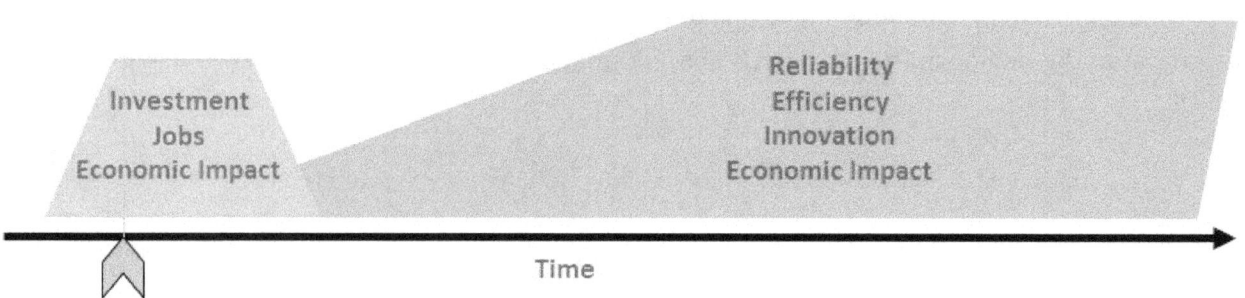

This analysis is aimed only at the short term economic benefits associated with the Smart Grid investments (green area in Figure 1), and does not attempt to assess the economic, operational, or societal benefits of a Smart Grid itself, which is the subject of longer-term DOE OE data collection and analysis, with public releases planned for 2013 and 2014. As Figure 1 above illustrates, the longer-term analysis will aim to capture the continuing impacts associated with reliability, efficiency, and innovation.

The short-term impacts associated with the ARRA Smart Grid project investments and the associated private sector matched investments are analyzed using the IMPLAN model, which estimates the economy wide impacts associated with two investment scenarios (defined below), relative to a scenario without any of these investments. Using IMPLAN, DOE estimated the 2012 economic impact of the investments on key economic indicators, including GDP, economic output, employment, labor income, and tax revenue.

Approach

Two different scenarios were formulated for economic analysis: the All Vendors Scenario and the Smart Grid Vendors Only Scenario.

- The **All Vendors Scenario** includes payments to core Smart Grid companies, as well as "non-core" vendors, such as accountants, temporary employment agencies, general purpose software and hardware vendors, and other goods and services required to accomplish grid modernization. The All Vendors Scenario also included the required industry matched investments, which were assumed to be equal to the federal payments—i.e., the total investment analyzed was two times the federal investment by itself.

- **The Smart Grid Vendors Only Scenario** is a subset of the All Vendors Scenario, and it includes federal payments made by SGIG and SGDP to core Smart Grid companies. These companies specifically deliver Smart Grid technologies, goods and services (such as advanced metering infrastructure, energy management systems, distribution automation, etc.). As with the All Vendors Scenario, industry-matched investments were also included.

Figure 2 – Investment Amounts for Analysis Scenarios

All Vendors Scenario

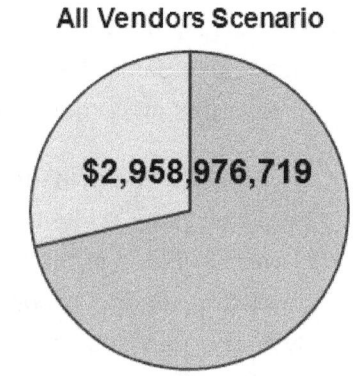

$2,958,976,719

Smart Grid Vendors Only Scenario

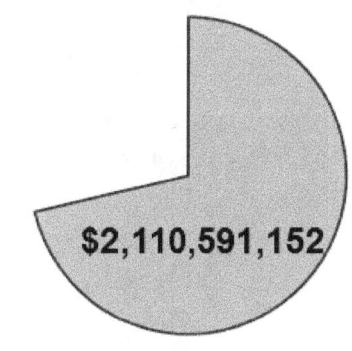

$2,110,591,152

The full breadth of the economy-wide benefits of the Smart Grid ARRA investment are analyzed in the All Vendors Scenario, while the Smart Grid Vendors Only Scenario allows for a more focused analysis of the Smart Grid core vendors and their labor-related and economic effects.

Both scenarios excluded any payments made by the Smart Grid ARRA awardees to their own employees as well as internal project expenses that did not result in vendor payments. Although these expenditures are relevant, this analysis was deliberately confined to publicly available data that reflects declared vendor payments. The result, however, is that this analysis does not capture awardees labor income or employment, and some portion of economic impact. It should also be noted that vendor payments of less than $25,000 were not required to be reported in www.Recovery.gov, and are not included in this analysis. Thus, the analysis potentially undercounts direct expenditures, and the analysis represents a conservative estimate of direct impacts.

Discussion of Smart Grid Vendors and Rationale

To create a list of core Smart Grid vendors, OE identified initial vendors from a previous list of companies compiled by the DOE in 2010,[1] and expanded the list to include Smart Grid vendors who attended major U.S. electric power and smart grid conferences or appeared in industry journals, major publications, or internet-based searches. Over 580 vendors were evaluated, about 400 of which were designated as core Smart Grid vendors and analyzed in more detail. Based on a vendor's corporate website, partner websites, and other related internet searches, the primary products and services that were marketed for Smart Grid related applications were identified and classified. In addition, relationships between a particular vendor and other Smart Grid related vendors were identified, based on analyzing partner lists on corporate websites, press releases and industry news.

The amount of ARRA related payments (under the SGIG and SGDP) to all vendors were derived from the www.Recovery.gov website. While the ARRA payments to vendors continue to date, only payments up to March 2012 were included in the analysis. Table 2 below lists the top 20 Smart Grid vendors out of a total of 117 Smart Grid vendors reported as receiving payments. Each vendor listed in Table 2 operates within an ecosystem of partners and suppliers that are not apparent in a top line analysis.

Table 2 – Top 20 Smart Grid Companies Receiving Smart Grid ARRA and Matching Funds

Company	ARRA Funds ($)
Itron	$304,828,804
Trilliant	$99,494,396
Accenture	$53,955,271
Honeywell	$50,856,201
GE	$44,646,429
Landis+Gyr	$44,388,260
Sensus	$38,900,498
IBM	$36,461,152
S&C Electric	$33,590,952
Alcatel-Lucent	$33,171,014
Elster	$30,223,339
Oracle	$26,730,073
Tantalus	$21,059,544
Black&Veatch	$19,787,742
Silver Spring Networks	$14,417,285
BPL Global	$12,728,072
ABB	$12,424,186
Grid One Solutions	$10,014,822
Cooper Power Systems	$8,964,545
Quanta Services	$8,646,263
Total (top 20)	$905,288,847

---

[1] http://energy.gov/oe/downloads/2010-us-smart-grid-vendor-ecosystem-report-companies-and-market-dynamics-shaping.

A review of the funded companies indicates that the majority of the Smart Grid vendors are publicly traded. In addition to the 117 core Smart Grid vendors, ARRA payments included a number of other non-core vendors that support the development and operation of the Smart Grid projects.

Introduction to IMPLAN

IMPLAN, a proprietary model maintained by the Minnesota IMPLAN Group (www.implan.com), is a widely used and effective regional economic analysis model that uses average expenditure data from industries. Expenditures in these industries "reverberate" up to the supplier industries; IMPLAN traces and calculates the multiple rounds of secondary indirect and induced economic impacts throughout the supply chain which remain in the selected region (see Figure 3). The regions can be the entire U.S., specific regions within the U.S., or various states. This Smart Grid analysis is conducted for the entire U.S.

Whenever new industry activity or income is injected into a selected regional economy (in this analysis, the entire U.S.), it initiates a "ripple" or multiplier effect that creates an economic impact that is often larger than the initial input. The multiplier effect is generated because the recipients of the new income spend some percentage of it in the region and the subsequent recipients of that income share, in turn, spend some share of it, and so on. The total spending impact of the new activity is the sum of these multiple, but progressively smaller, rounds of spending within the local economy. This additional economic activity creates new local economic activity, jobs (i.e., the total employment), and tax revenues for federal and state/local governments (i.e., the total fiscal impact).

For this analysis, DOE used the most recent version of IMPLAN (Version 3.0) model with a national-level data set. IMPLAN Version 3.0 uses 2010 data and improves on previous versions of the model by implementing a methodology for estimating regional imports and exports.

The IMPLAN model is based on the input-output data from the U.S. National Income and Product Accounts (NIPA) from the Bureau of Economic Analysis. The model includes 440 economic sectors based on the North American Industry Classification System (NAICS). The model uses region-specific multipliers to trace and calculate the flow of dollars from the industries that originate the economic activity to supplier industries that generate additional activity (as noted above). These multipliers are thus coefficients that "describe the response of the economy to a stimulus (a change in demand or production)." Figure 3 below illustrates the three types of impacts used in IMPLAN:

- **Direct** – represents the economic impacts (e.g., employment or output changes) due to the direct investments, such as payments to companies in Smart Grid 'core' industries.
- **Indirect** – represents the economic impacts due to the industry inter-linkages caused by the iteration of industries purchasing from industries, brought about by the changes in final demands (e.g., when a meter manufacturer purchases computer chips from another company).
- **Induced** – represents the economic impacts on all local industries due to consumers' consumption expenditures arising from the new household incomes that are generated by the direct and indirect effects of the final demand changes (e.g., a worker purchases new clothing or purchases food in restaurants).

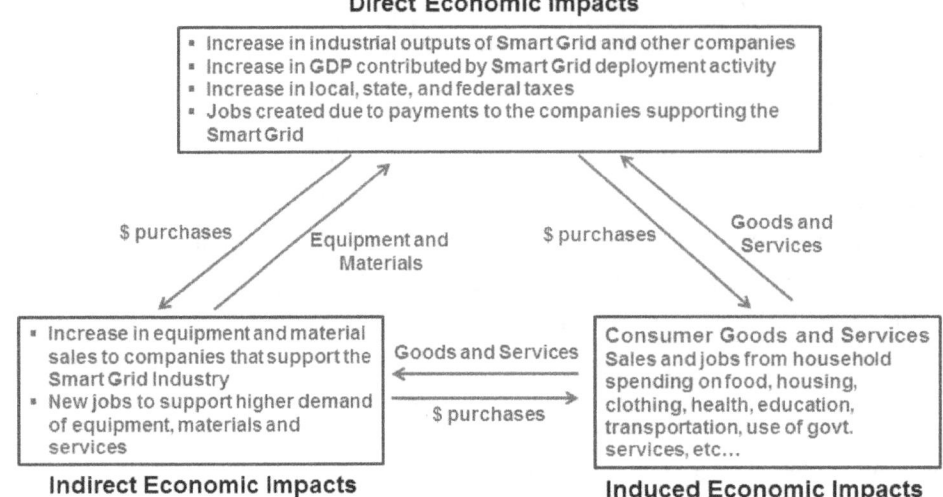

The total impact is simply the sum of the direct and the multiple rounds of secondary indirect and induced impacts that remain in the region (the entire U.S. in this case). IMPLAN then uses this total impact to calculate subsequent impacts such as total jobs created and tax impacts. This methodology, and the use of IMPLAN, is well-established and consistent with numerous other studies of national policy.

DOE used IMPLAN default information for each industry's local purchase coefficients (LPC). The LPC accounts for spending "leakages" outside the modeling region, in this case the entire U.S. For example, an industry that relies heavily on imported raw materials or non-U.S. labor will have a lower LPC, meaning that direct spending and subsequent rounds of economic impact in that industry will "leak" outside of the nation.

The leakage value accounts for economic activity occurring outside of the U.S. as result of ARRA support for Smart Grid. For this analysis, the use of the IMPLAN default LPCs might overestimate the leakages, because results indicate that the most significant leakages occur during direct spending. Thus, DOE's analysis provides a more conservative estimate of the total impact in the U.S.

Modeling Approach

Model Inputs

The first step to conducting the impact modeling was to define the economic inputs stimuli for two different scenarios considered in this analysis. As discussed above, the inputs are based on actual SGIG and SGDP payments to vendors, as reported in www.Recovery.gov.

For the Smart Grid Vendors Only Scenario, direct payments made only to core Smart Grid vendors (and matching industry funds) were used as input to the model. For the All Vendors Scenario, payments to core Smart Grid as well as "non-core" vendors (and the total associated matching industry funds) were included as input to the model.

Next, each vendor was matched to the relevant industry code, based on NAICS codes. DOE obtained the primary NAICS codes for nearly 300 core Smart Grid vendors (mostly based on data from INFOUSA and additional analysis). Using these NAICS codes, and mapping between NAICS code and IMPLAN sectors, DOE mapped the relevant vendors to IMPLAN sectors. The Smart Grid vendors with NAICS code were mapped to 33 IMPLAN sectors, about 8% of total IMPLAN sectors. This implies that the Smart Grid industry has a diverse set of companies/vendors with a significant footprint in the U.S. economy. The input dollar amounts for the various IMPLAN sectors are shown in Appendix A.

Model Outputs

Once the data was prepared for input into IMPLAN, DOE ran the model for each scenario and generated the outputs. Outputs were reported for the direct, indirect, and induced impacts under each scenario in terms of employment, labor income, GDP, total economic output, and state/local and federal tax revenue. The sector level output for employment is shown in Appendix B.

Findings

Summary

The summary table below (Table 4) presents the results for each scenario in terms of employment, total labor income, GDP and economic output impacts. Labor income is the value of all forms of employment income, including employee compensation (wages and benefits) and proprietor (owner) income. GDP is the market value of the goods and services produced by labor and property located within the borders of the United States. It is one of the best indicators of a program's impact as it captures value-added impact, i.e., it is equal to its gross output (which consists of sales or receipts and other operating income, commodity taxes, and inventory change) minus its intermediate inputs (which consist of energy, raw materials, semi-finished goods, and services) that are purchased from domestic industries or from foreign sources. In comparison, economic output represents the total value of industry production or in basic terms the value of each industry's sales.

Table 4 – Summary Results

	Total Impact	
	All Vendors	**Smart Grid Vendors**
Employment (jobs)	47,000	33,000
Labor Income (2010$)	$2.86 Billion	$2.07 Billion
GDP (2010$)	$4.18 Billion	$2.91 Billion
Economic Output (2010$)	$6.83 Billion	$4.79 Billion
State and Local taxes (2010$)	$0.36 Billion	$0.26 Billion
Federal taxes (2010$)	$0.66 Billion	$0.49 Billion

The results indicate that ARRA Smart Grid program investment generated significant benefits to the U.S. economy. For the All Vendors Scenario, $2.96 billion in payments, which was comprised of $1.48 billion of ARRA funding and $1.48 billion in private sector matching funds, generated $6.83 billion in total economic output. The Smart Grid Vendors Only Scenario generated payments of $2.11 billion, which was comprised of $1.05 billion of ARRA funding and $1.05 billion in private sector match funds, generated $4.79 billion in total economic output.

Positive impacts on labor income and employment occurred throughout the U.S. economy. In the All Vendors Scenario, 47,000 jobs were supported. The findings indicate that investment in core Smart Grid industries supports higher paying jobs compared to other non-core industries impacted by Smart Grid ARRA support. This is based on the fact that the average labor income in the Smart Grid Vendors Only Scenario is higher than the All Vendors Scenario, both of which exceed average income observed in the supply chain and the general economy. Industrial sectors that benefited directly from ARRA support include computer systems design, technical and scientific services and consulting, and electrical/wireless equipment and component manufacturing. These high impact sectors indirectly benefit and induce growth in real estate, wholesale trade, financial services, restaurants, and health care sectors.

DOE also calculated the GDP multiplier associated with each scenario. For every $1 million of direct spending, which includes both ARRA and private sector matching funds, the GDP increased by $2.5 to $2.6 million. This "Smart Grid" GDP multiplier is higher than many forms of government investments and is also higher than direct transfer to individuals.

Discussion by Indicator

The following sections describe in more detail the results of the analysis.

GDP

GDP is one of the best indicators of a program's impact as it captures the net value (value-added) associated with the investment. As can be seen in Figure 4, the All Vendors Scenario contributes $4.18 billion to the nation's GDP, with the Smart Grid Vendors Only Scenario contributing $2.91 billion. The amplifying effect of the direct effect versus total economic effect is termed a "GDP multiplier," and is often used to compare investment alternatives.

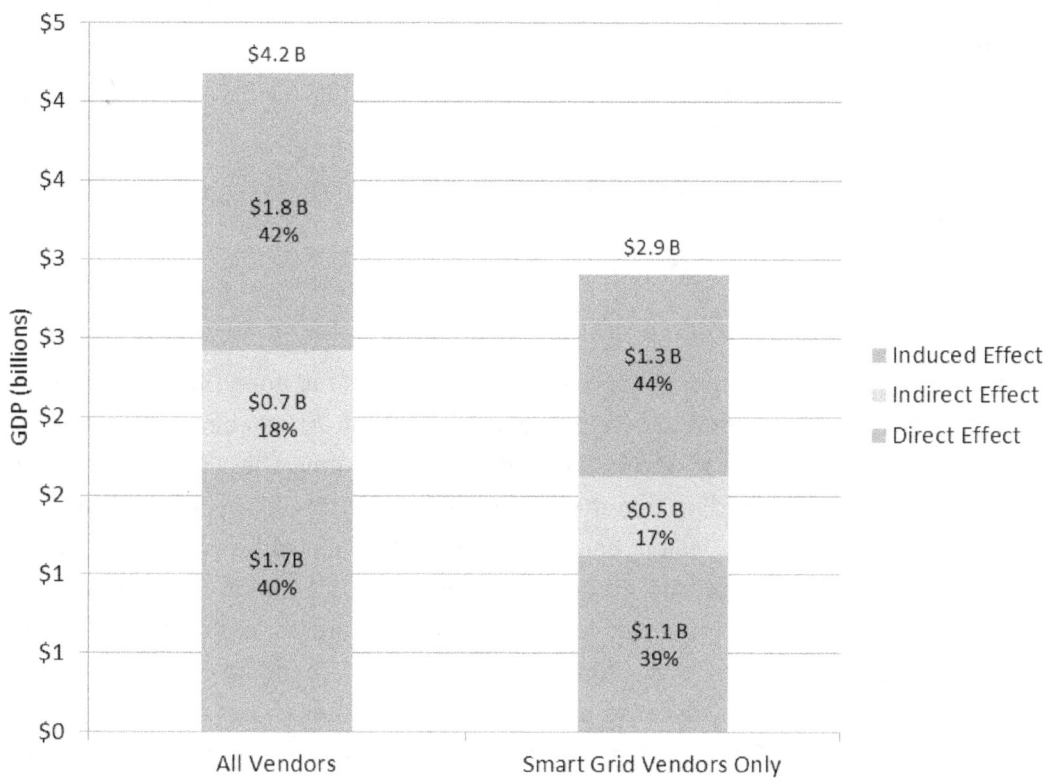

Figure 4 – Smart Grid ARRA Support's Impact on Gross Domestic Product

Percentages may not equal 100% due to rounding

A GDP multiplier is often used to compare investment alternatives by measuring the value of the output compared to the input, or in other words the "bang for the buck" of a policy or program. For the All Vendors Scenario, for every $1 million of direct spending, the GDP grew by $2.5 million (i.e., a GDP multiplier of 2.5), and for the Smart Grid Vendors Only Scenario, the GDP increased by $2.6 million. Direct spending in this case includes the sum of both ARRA and private sector matching funds.

The Congressional Budget Office published estimates of the GDP multipliers associated with various types of public spending. As can be seen in Table 5, both ARRA Smart Grid scenarios have slightly higher GDP multipliers compared to the maximum achieved (or similar) multipliers from government procurement programs, state/local infrastructure projects, other state/local programs, or direct payments to citizens. This is a significant finding, as it means that for every dollar invested in the ARRA Smart Grid programs, the resulting impact was higher or comparable to other investment opportunities. This result, coupled with the long term benefits of Smart Grid deployment, which include increases in reliability, electrical distribution and transmission efficiency, operational efficiency, and flexibility that enable a more diverse energy portfolio, makes a strong case for continued Smart Grid deployment investment.

Table 5 - Comparison of GDP Multipliers

Type of Activity	Output Multiplier
All Vendors Scenario	2.5
Smart Grid Vendors Only Scenario	2.6
Purchases of Goods and Services by the Federal Government	1.0-2.5
Transfer of Payments to State and Local Governments for Infrastructure	1.0-2.5
Transfer of Payments to State and Local Governments for Other Purposes	0.7-1.9
Transfer of Payments to Individuals	0.8-2.2

Source: ICF/IMPLAN; Congressional Budget Office (CBO)

Output

Economic output is another commonly used standard measure for analyzing economic impact, as it includes all economic activity generated by a policy or investment. As can be seen in Figure 5, the ARRA Smart Grid program contributed at least $6.83 billion to the economy. The direct effect, signified in dark green, represents the direct spending under each scenario. The direct spending of $2.6 billion is less than the input amount of $2.96 billion because of leakage, i.e., some of the economic output is occurring outside the U.S. Based on the modeling, as much as $1.1 billion of economic output occurs outside the U.S. due to leakages. However, nearly $400 million are estimated to be leaked during the direct spending round, which is an overestimation as the direct spending for this program is in U.S.-based companies. As noted above, because of this difference between how ARRA funds were actually used and the default modeling framework, the total estimated leakage is likely higher than in actuality.

Figure 5 - Smart Grid ARRA Support's Impact on Economic Output

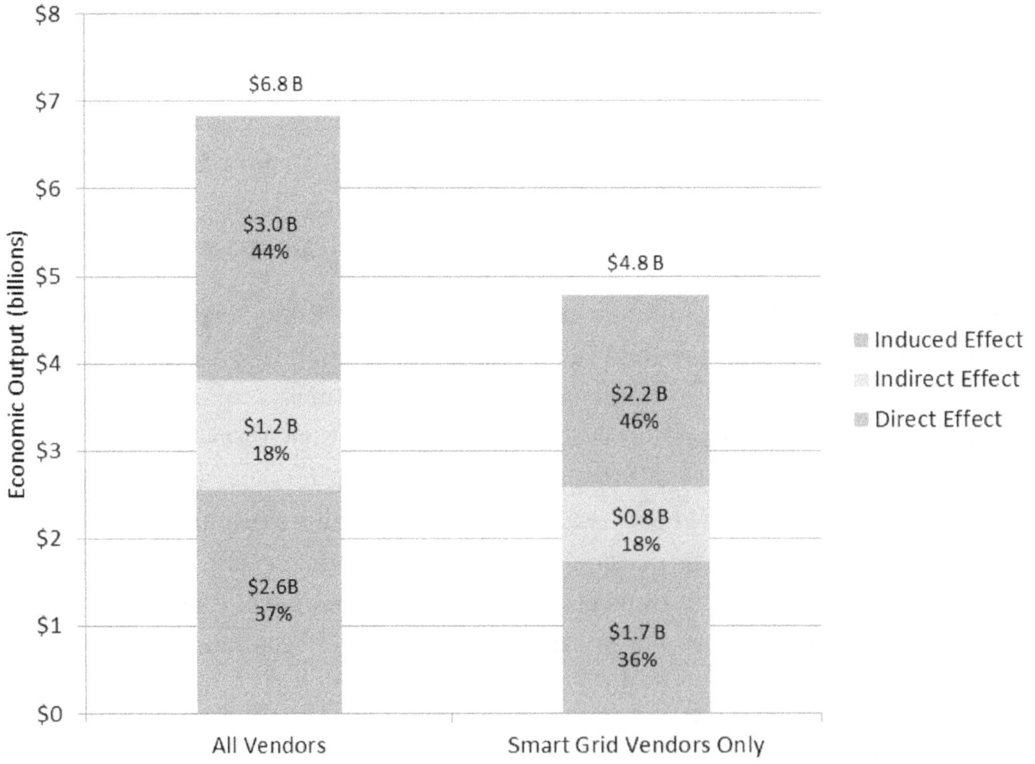

Percentages may not equal 100% due to rounding

Employment is probably the most commonly understood metric of economic impact, and was one of the clear policy missions for the entire ARRA program. As can be seen in Figure 6, the ARRA Smart Grid program supported at least 47,000 jobs. (As mentioned above in the Approach section, jobs of grant recipients' employees are not captured, and result in some undercounting.) The direct jobs, signified in dark green, represent the direct employment in the various companies. In the All Vendors Scenario, 18,000 jobs were supported by direct investment, with 29,000 jobs being supported by indirect and induced economic activities. In the Smart Grid Vendors Only Scenario, 12,000 jobs were supported directly, 6,000 indirect jobs in their respective supply chains. Given the mission of DOE OE to sustain and accelerate the pace of grid modernization in the U.S., employment and other economic impacts in the core Smart Grid vendor base is an important effect, as these organizations are critical to projects that follow. Smart Grid ARRA funding supported employment in a variety of sectors, including over 10,000 jobs in professional and technical services, which includes industry sectors such as computer systems design, management and technical consulting, architecture and engineering services. The Smart Grid ARRA program also supported more than 2,500 jobs in the food, drink, and restaurant industry, 1,500 jobs in both the health care and real estate services sectors, and roughly 1,000 jobs in both the financial services and high-end manufacturing industries. Employment in service industries such as health care and food services is almost entirely due to the induced impact, as higher wages in core and value-chain Smart Grid vendors increase demand for consumer spending.

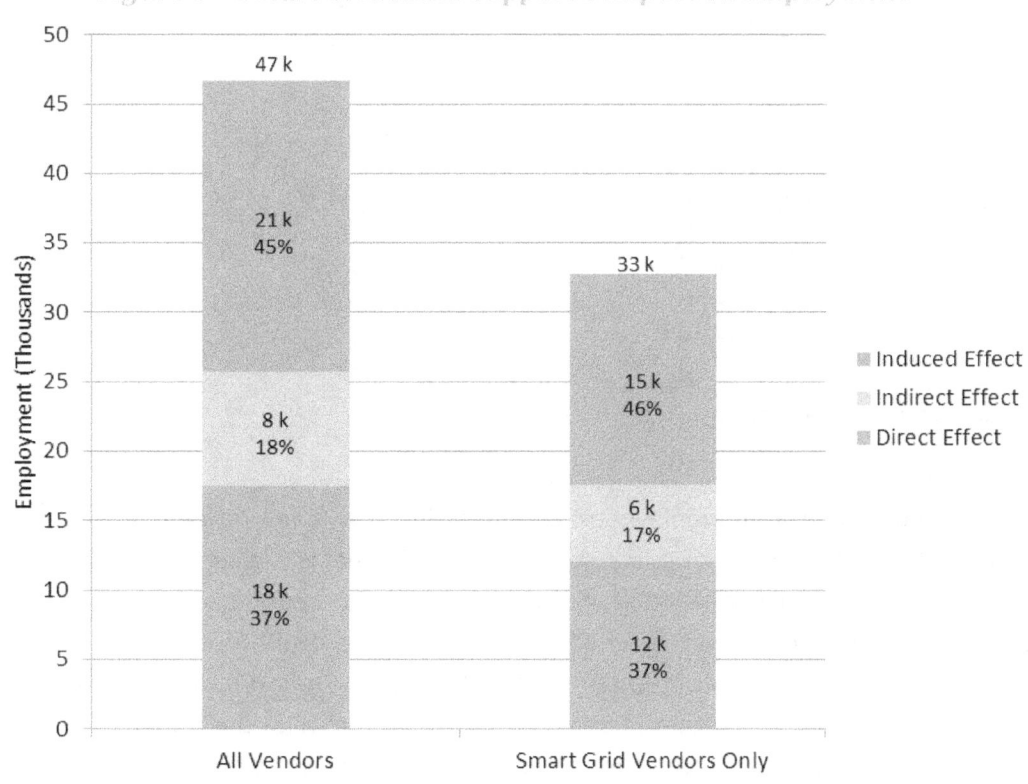

Figure 6 – Smart Grid ARRA Support's Impact on Employment

Percentages may not equal 100% due to rounding

13

Labor income impacts account for the total wages generated across all industries as a result of ARRA Smart Grid program spending. As can be seen in Figure 7 below, the ARRA Smart Grid program impacted labor income by contributing at least $2.86 billion. In the Smart Grid Vendors Only Scenario, $2.1 billion in vendor payments resulted in an estimated $1.1 billion in labor income within those companies, and an additional $0.3 billion in their respective supply chains. Key industrial sectors included computer systems design, technical and scientific services and consulting, and electrical equipment and components, among others.

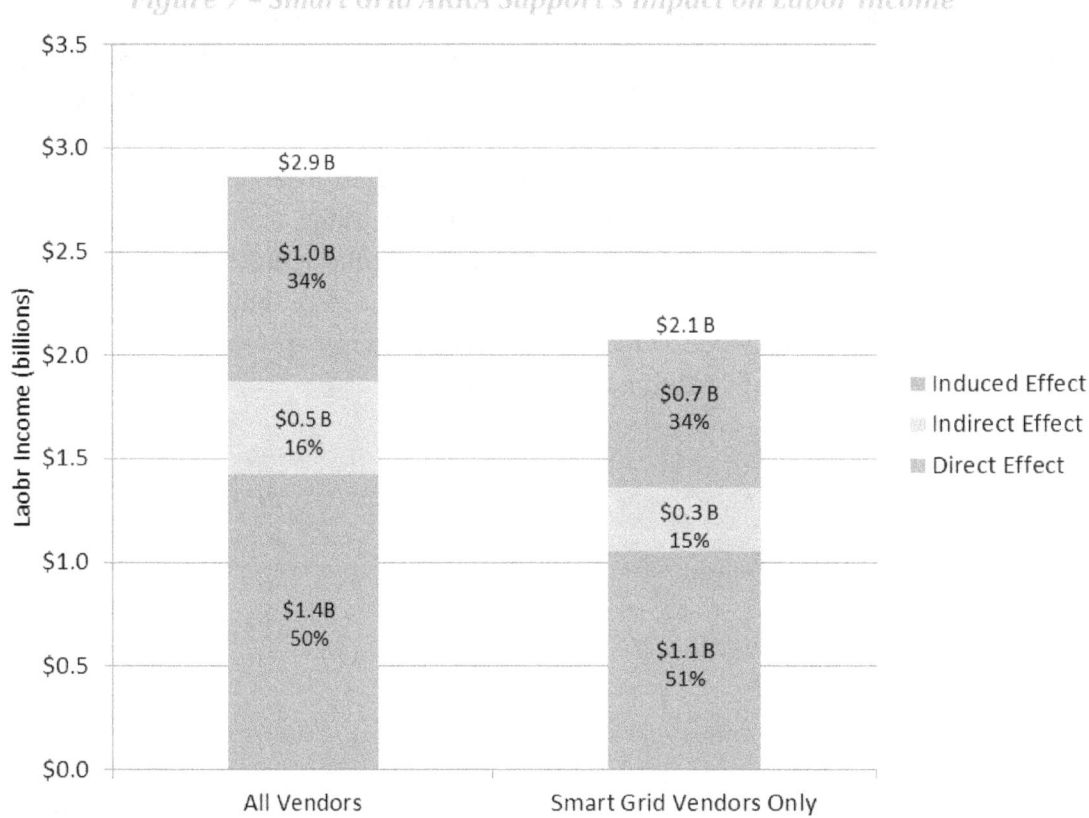

Figure 7 – Smart Grid ARRA Support's Impact on Labor Income

Percentages may not equal 100% due to rounding

Combining the information from employment and labor income, it can be seen in Figure 8 below that the Smart Grid Vendors Only Scenario is associated with noticeably higher direct income, and slightly higher incomes for indirect labor, which suggests that Smart Grid core jobs pay slightly higher wages than average U.S. jobs, which is represented by the composite of all types of vendors necessary to accomplish a Smart Grid project, represented by the All Vendors Scenario). Average per-worker income in both scenarios is roughly 35% higher in Smart Grid core sectors than the broader sectors included in indirect and induced effects. This trend is in part due to the fact that manufacturing, research and development, and professional service jobs, which comprise the occupations in the direct and indirect sectors, are higher paying than service sectors jobs, which are typically found in the broader U.S. economy.

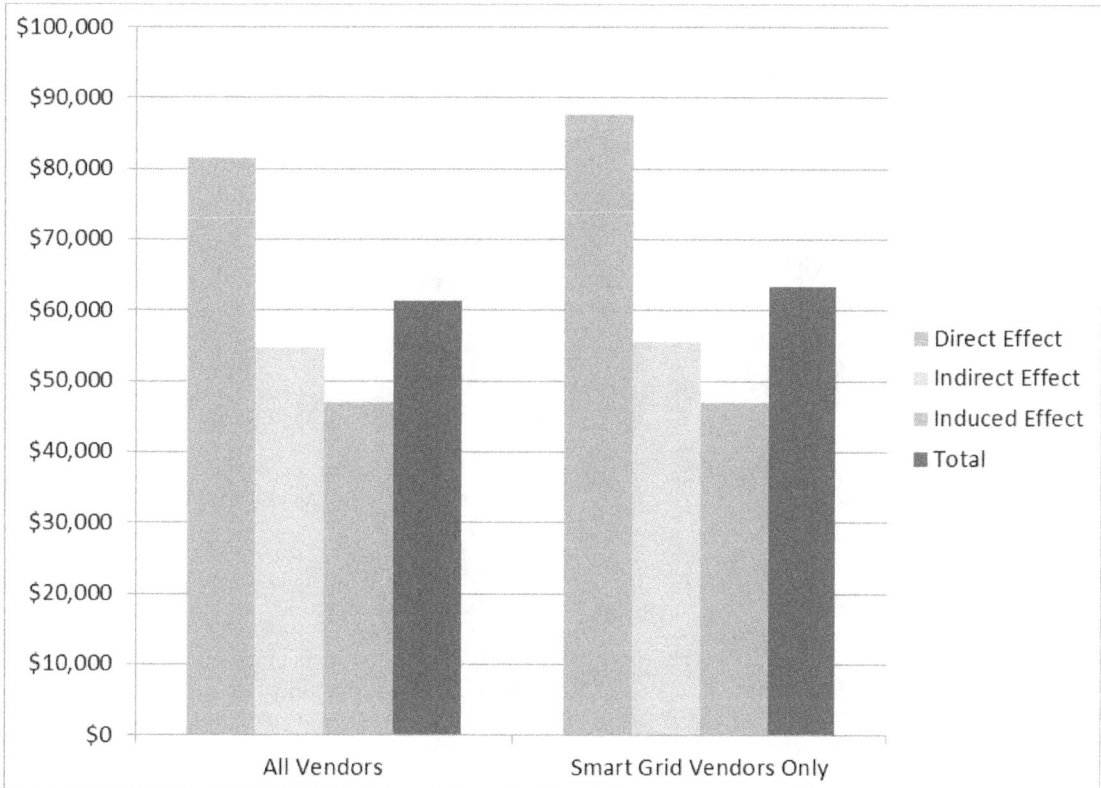

Figure 8 – Labor Per-Worker Income Comparison

The ARRA Smart Grid program expenditures by the federal government also generate federal, state and local tax revenue. As can be seen in Figure 9 below, the ARRA Smart Grid program generated more than $1 billion in tax revenues under the All Vendors Scenario, almost $748 million of which is attributable to Smart Grid vendors. Building a smarter grid requires expertise and organizations in energy, information technology, logistics, and communications, among others. As a result, vendors are more geographically dispersed than other "high tech" industries. Correspondingly, the $361 million in state and local tax revenue is dispersed across a larger portion of the nation as well. At the state/local level, the most significant revenues are generated by sales and property taxes. These taxes are a result of direct, indirect, and induced economic impacts from the Smart Grid investments.

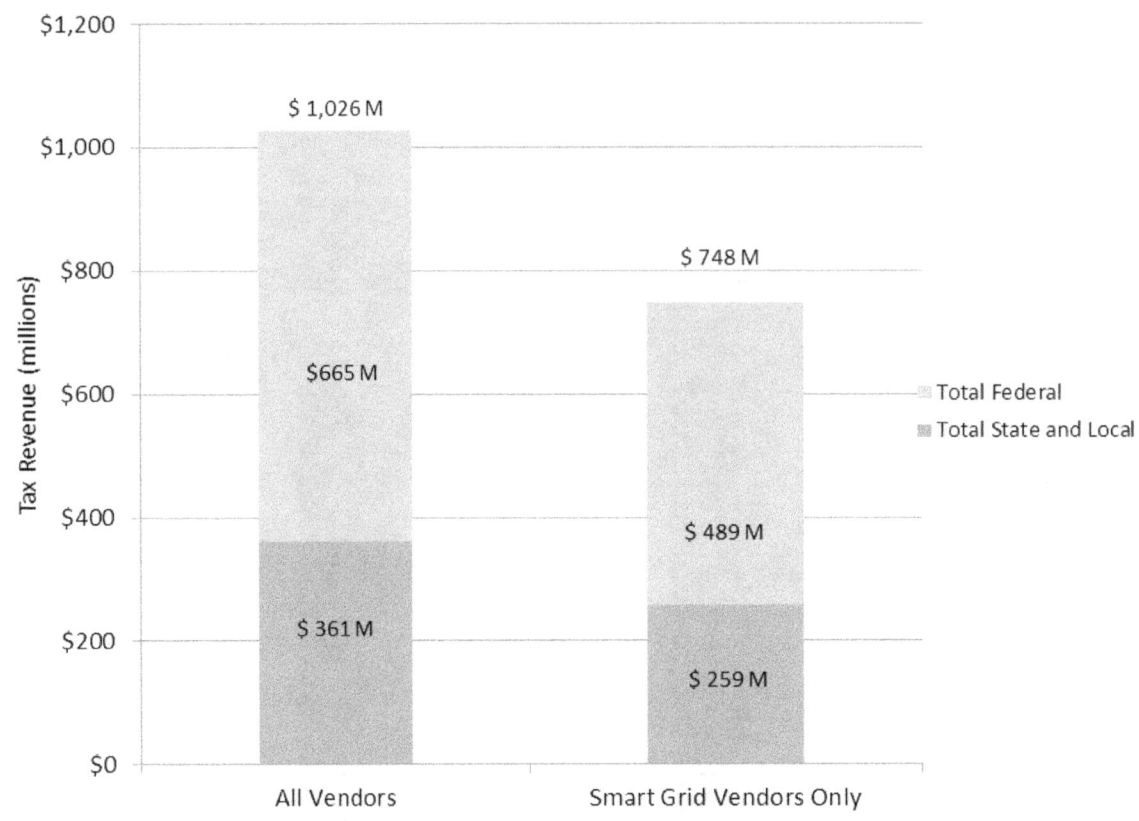

Figure 9 – Smart Grid ARRA Support's Impact on Tax Revenue

Analysis Conclusions

It is clear from this analysis that Smart Grid ARRA funding, alongside active financial and material participation by utilities, high tech companies, and their labor forces, generates a markedly positive impact on the U.S. economy. Given the nature of Smart Grid projects, follow-on investments funded by state and private sector sources are likely to have a similar positive impact profile.

This analysis has only analyzed a portion of the total ARRA Smart Grid investment. It indicates that the investment, of $2.96 billion to pursue grid modernization, generated at least $6.8 billion in total economic output. In addition, at least 47,000 total jobs were supported as a result of Smart Grid ARRA investments. Key industrial sectors that were directly impacted include: computer systems design, technical and scientific services and consulting, and electrical/wireless equipment, and component manufacturing. Indirect and induced sectors include: real estate, wholesale trade, financial services, restaurants, and health care.

Furthermore, for every $1 million of direct spending (government + matching), GDP expanded by $2.5-2.6 million. The "GDP multiplier" of 2.5 for the All Vendors Scenario, and a multiplier of 2.6 for the Smart Grid Vendors Only Scenario, compares favorably to other forms of investment, including defense, other infrastructure and general acquisition.

While analysis accounts for the $1.48 billion in Smart Grid ARRA funds (along with $1.48 billion in private sector matching funds), the ARRA programs are still underway and an additional $2.5 billion of federal and $4.1 billion of private sector funds will be spent by the time both programs end.

Comment on the Mission Objective Grid Modernization

Since the Energy Independence and Security Act of 2007, it has been the policy of the United States to modernize its electricity infrastructure for the economic well-being and security of the nation. By the conclusion of both the Smart Grid Investment Grant and Smart Grid Demonstration programs, $9.56 billion will have been spent by the federal government and the private sector. This investment in Smart Grid deployment must serve as a catalyst to sustain the pace of modernization, while improving the economic and operational benefits of such investments in the coming years. As indicated in Figure 10 below, the amount of investment needed for full Smart Grid deployment is significantly larger than the ARRA investments. Such large scale investments will continue to contribute significant employment and economic benefits to the U.S. economy.

Figure 10 – Required Smart Grid Investments

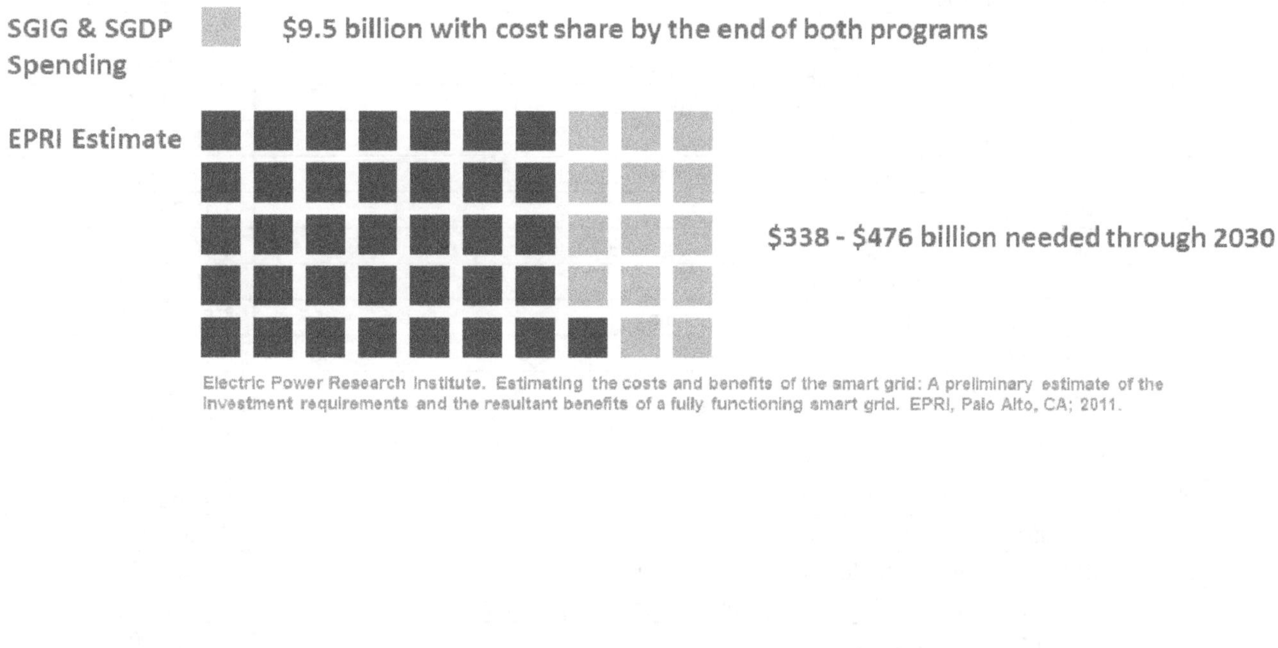

SGIG & SGDP Spending $9.5 billion with cost share by the end of both programs

EPRI Estimate

$338 - $476 billion needed through 2030

Electric Power Research Institute. Estimating the costs and benefits of the smart grid: A preliminary estimate of the investment requirements and the resultant benefits of a fully functioning smart grid. EPRI, Palo Alto, CA; 2011.

The tables in Appendix A provide the amount of input dollars for the relevant IMPLAN sectors. The grayscale rows in the All Vendors Scenarios are those sectors that are not in the Smart Grid Vendors Only Scenario (see below). Input includes federal and matching funds.

All Vendors Scenario

Sector	IMPLAN Description	Input ($)
372	Computer systems design services	$ 548,123,115
380	All other miscellaneous professional, scientific, and technical services	$ 489,710,913
374	Management, scientific, and technical consulting services	$ 456,380,269
389	Other support services	$ 220,394,672
275	All other miscellaneous electrical equipment and component manufacturing	$ 213,334,266
247	Other electronic component manufacturing	$ 166,672,933
238	Broadcast and wireless communications equipment	$ 164,590,316
369	Architectural, engineering, and related services	$ 143,679,426
319	Wholesale trade	$ 111,065,889
345	Software publishers	$ 98,469,751
373	Other computer related services, including facilities management	$ 96,565,424
268	Switchgear and switchboard apparatus manufacturing	$ 63,498,980
36	Construction of other new nonresidential structures	$ 39,136,784
371	Custom computer programming services	$ 35,744,116
31	Electric power generation, transmission, and distribution	$ 21,247,297
351	Telecommunications	$ 18,700,250
272	Communication and energy wire and cable manufacturing	$ 14,087,764
270	Storage battery manufacturing	$ 10,492,938
239	Other communications equipment manufacturing	$ 5,504,558
393	Other educational services	$ 5,381,210
271	Primary battery manufacturing	$ 5,354,932
367	Legal services	$ 5,343,773
352	Data processing, hosting, and related services	$ 5,179,261
269	Relay and industrial control manufacturing	$ 4,662,432
376	Scientific research and development services	$ 3,034,313
244	Electronic capacitor, resistor, coil, transformer, and other inductor manufacturing	$ 2,539,453
236	Computer terminals and other computer peripheral equipment manufacturing	$ 2,499,344
171	Steel product manufacturing from purchased steel	$ 1,682,900
234	Electronic computer manufacturing	$ 1,565,968
368	Accounting, tax preparation, bookkeeping, and payroll services	$ 1,332,464
251	Industrial process variable instruments manufacturing	$ 1,049,020
265	Other major household appliance manufacturing	$ 1,045,205
266	Power, distribution, and specialty transformer manufacturing	$ 624,247
353	Data processing, hosting, and related services	$ 157,640
250	Automatic environmental control manufacturing	$ 124,898
TOTAL		$ 2,958,976,719

Smart Grid Vendors Only Scenario

IMPLAN	IMPLAN Description	Input (spending $)
372	Computer systems design services	$ 513,959,678
380	All other miscellaneous professional, scientific, and technical services	$ 365,715,573
374	Management, scientific, and technical consulting services	$ 304,833,665
275	All other miscellaneous electrical equipment and component manufacturing	$ 240,330,185
247	Other electronic component manufacturing	$ 157,283,816
238	Broadcast and wireless communications equipment	$ 129,153,916
373	Other computer related services, including facilities management	$ 99,716,979
369	Architectural, engineering, and related services	$ 89,413,077
268	Switchgear and switchboard apparatus manufacturing	$ 60,858,809
371	Custom computer programming services	$ 33,235,786
31	Electric power generation, transmission, and distribution	$ 20,386,870
345	Software publishers	$ 20,017,741
389	Other support services	$ 18,229,463
36	Construction of other new nonresidential structures	$ 14,697,497
351	Telecommunications	$ 10,531,237
270	Storage battery manufacturing	$ 9,466,084
239	Other communications equipment manufacturing	$ 5,504,558
352	Data processing, hosting, and related services	$ 5,179,261
319	Wholesale Trade	$ 4,245,541
244	Electronic capacitor, resistor, coil, transformer, and other inductor manufacturing	$ 2,539,453
234	Electronic computer manufacturing	$ 1,565,968
236	Computer terminals and other computer peripheral equipment manufacturing	$ 1,507,573
265	Other major household appliance manufacturing	$ 1,004,566
266	Power, distribution, and specialty transformer manufacturing	$ 664,885
269	Relay and industrial control manufacturing	$ 266,433
353	Data processing, hosting, and related services	$ 157,640
250	Automatic environmental control manufacturing	$ 124,898
TOTAL		$ 2,110,591,152

The tables in Appendix B show the sector-level employment impacts (for all sectors with more than 50 jobs). The grayscale sectors are those that received no direct funding.

All Vendors Scenario

Sector	Sector Description	Direct	Indirect	Induced	Total
372	Computer systems design services	5,941	127	64	6,132
374	Management, scientific, and technical consulting services	3,264	284	157	3,705
413	Food services and drinking places	0	794	2,128	2,922
380	All other miscellaneous professional, scientific, and technical services	2,119	94	44	2,256
389	Other support services	2,023	94	45	2,162
319	Wholesale trade businesses	666	379	726	1,771
360	Real estate establishments	0	510	1,170	1,681
369	Architectural, engineering, and related services	1,133	290	85	1,508
382	Employment services	0	1,033	466	1,499
247	Other electronic component manufacturing	954	72	3	1,029
394	Offices of physicians, dentists, and other health practitioners	0	0	1,011	1,011
397	Private hospitals	0	0	981	981
275	All other miscellaneous electrical equipment and component manufacturing	891	18	1	910
356	Securities, commodity contracts, investments, and related activities	0	148	602	750
355	Nondepository credit intermediation and related activities	0	182	549	732
388	Services to buildings and dwellings	0	364	358	722
398	Nursing and residential care facilities	0	0	686	686
329	Retail Stores - General merchandise	0	8	657	664
324	Retail Stores - Food and beverage	0	8	656	664
381	Management of companies and enterprises	0	339	207	546
426	Private household operations	0	0	520	520
368	Accounting, tax preparation, bookkeeping, and payroll services	11	315	187	514
367	Legal services	31	214	261	506
425	Civic, social, professional, and similar organizations	0	93	384	477
354	Monetary authorities and depository credit intermediation activities	0	177	300	477
373	Other computer related services, including facilities management	376	54	19	449
357	Insurance carriers	0	89	313	402
320	Retail Stores - Motor vehicle and parts	0	8	393	401
400	Individual and family services	0	0	392	392

Sector	Sector Description	Direct	Indirect	Induced	Total
411	Hotels and motels, including casino hotels	0	183	196	380
386	Business support services	0	232	144	376
331	Retail Nonstores - Direct and electronic sales	0	3	350	354
238	Broadcast and wireless communications equipment manufacturing	328	17	1	347
327	Retail Stores - Clothing and clothing accessories	0	4	342	346
351	Telecommunications	39	140	148	326
371	Custom computer programming services	271	40	16	326
393	Other private educational services	92	4	225	321
330	Retail Stores - Miscellaneous	0	4	312	316
358	Insurance agencies, brokerages, and related activities	0	81	233	314
335	Transport by truck	0	95	209	304
392	Private junior colleges, colleges, universities, and professional schools	0	4	289	293
395	Home health care services	0	0	281	281
396	Medical and diagnostic labs and outpatient and other ambulatory care services	0	1	279	280
414	Automotive repair and maintenance, except car washes	0	67	211	278
377	Advertising and related services	0	160	114	274
39	Maintenance and repair construction of nonresidential structures	0	112	159	271
345	Software publishers	217	39	15	271
387	Investigation and security services	0	152	116	267
36	Construction of other new nonresidential structures	266	0	0	266
399	Child day care services	0	0	261	261
325	Retail Stores - Health and personal care	0	3	247	250
391	Private elementary and secondary schools	0	0	248	248
419	Personal care services	0	0	217	217
340	Warehousing and storage	0	108	103	211
427	US Postal Service	0	103	99	202
339	Couriers and messengers	0	113	87	201
323	Retail Stores - Building material and garden supply	0	5	193	198
384	Office administrative services	0	134	63	197
336	Transit and ground passenger transportation	0	93	104	196
376	Scientific research and development services	17	117	60	193
268	Switchgear and switchboard apparatus manufacturing	181	10	1	192
409	Amusement parks, arcades, and gambling industries	0	1	177	178
424	Grantmaking, giving, and social advocacy organizations	0	0	175	175
326	Retail Stores - Gasoline stations	0	3	172	175
328	Retail Stores - Sporting goods, hobby, book and music	0	2	168	169
432	Other state and local government enterprises	0	25	144	168
113	Printing	0	94	66	160

Sector	Sector Description	Direct	Indirect	Induced	Total
407	Fitness and recreational sports centers	0	46	110	156
402	Performing arts companies	0	55	97	152
401	Community food, housing, and other relief services, including rehabilitation services	0	0	149	149
403	Spectator sports companies	0	54	93	146
410	Other amusement and recreation industries	0	32	105	137
404	Promoters of performing arts and sports and agents for public figures	0	36	98	133
338	Scenic and sightseeing transportation and support activities for transportation	0	59	70	130
31	Electric power generation, transmission, and distribution	34	26	67	127
322	Retail Stores - Electronics and appliances	0	1	118	120
370	Specialized design services	0	100	18	118
20	Extraction of oil and natural gas	0	27	91	118
321	Retail Stores - Furniture and home furnishings	0	1	111	112
346	Motion picture and video industries	0	53	57	111
421	Dry-cleaning and laundry services	0	19	91	111
423	Religious organizations	0	0	100	100
422	Other personal services	0	13	87	99
2	Grain farming	0	7	88	96
332	Transport by air	0	35	60	95
341	Newspaper publishers	0	44	50	93
359	Funds, trusts, and other financial vehicles	0	2	90	92
417	Commercial and industrial machinery and equipment repair and maintenance	0	47	43	90
19	Support activities for agriculture and forestry	0	7	83	89
348	Radio and television broadcasting	0	48	36	84
352	Data processing, hosting, ISP, web search portals and related services	16	17	43	77
390	Waste management and remediation services	0	24	49	74
14	Animal production, except cattle and poultry and eggs	0	3	70	74
430	State and local government passenger transit	0	35	39	74
379	Veterinary services	0	0	72	73
383	Travel arrangement and reservation services	0	43	29	72
195	Machine shops	0	51	18	69
243	Semiconductor and related device manufacturing	0	60	9	69
362	Automotive equipment rental and leasing	0	26	36	63
11	Cattle ranching and farming	0	2	59	61
375	Environmental and other technical consulting services	0	39	19	58
283	Motor vehicle parts manufacturing	0	17	38	55
405	Independent artists, writers, and performers	0	27	27	54

Sector	Sector Description	Direct	Indirect	Induced	Total
363	General and consumer goods rental except video tapes and discs	0	8	45	53
415	Car washes	0	6	45	51
TOTAL		**19,005**	**9,851**	**23,712**	**52,569**

Smart Grid Vendors Only Scenario

Sector	Sector Description	Direct	Indirect	Induced	Total
372	Computer systems design services	5,543	76	41	5,661
374	Management, scientific, and technical consulting services	2,107	163	101	2,370
413	Food services and drinking places	0	510	1,367	1,876
380	All other miscellaneous professional, scientific, and technical services	1,573	60	28	1,661
360	Real estate establishments	0	301	750	1,051
369	Architectural, engineering, and related services	698	203	55	956
382	Employment services	0	586	300	885
319	Wholesale trade businesses	26	168	465	658
394	Offices of physicians, dentists, and other health practitioners	0	0	649	649
397	Private hospitals	0	0	630	630
247	Other electronic component manufacturing	493	29	2	524
356	Securities, commodity contracts, investments, and related activities	0	86	386	472
355	Nondepository credit intermediation and related activities	0	100	353	453
398	Nursing and residential care facilities	0	0	441	441
388	Services to buildings and dwellings	0	207	230	437
373	Other computer related services, including facilities management	381	37	12	430
329	Retail Stores - General merchandise	0	4	422	426
324	Retail Stores - Food and beverage	0	4	422	426
275	All other miscellaneous electrical equipment and component manufacturing	353	7	0	360
426	Private household operations	0	0	336	336
368	Accounting, tax preparation, bookkeeping, and payroll services	0	189	120	309
354	Monetary authorities and depository credit intermediation activities	0	114	193	306
425	Civic, social, professional, and similar organizations	0	58	247	305
381	Management of companies and enterprises	0	158	133	291
367	Legal services	0	122	168	290
371	Custom computer programming services	249	21	10	280
320	Retail Stores - Motor vehicle and parts	0	4	253	257
411	Hotels and motels, including casino hotels	0	126	126	253

Sector	Sector Description	Direct	Indirect	Induced	Total
357	Insurance carriers	0	51	201	252
400	Individual and family services	0	0	252	252
389	Other support services	167	48	29	244
331	Retail Nonstores - Direct and electronic sales	0	2	225	227
327	Retail Stores - Clothing and clothing accessories	0	2	220	222
386	Business support services	0	125	92	217
330	Retail Stores - Miscellaneous	0	2	201	203
351	Telecommunications	22	85	95	201
358	Insurance agencies, brokerages, and related activities	0	45	150	195
392	Private junior colleges, colleges, universities, and professional schools	0	3	186	189
335	Transport by truck	0	46	135	181
395	Home health care services	0	0	181	181
396	Medical and diagnostic labs and outpatient and other ambulatory care services	0	0	179	179
414	Automotive repair and maintenance, except car washes	0	35	135	170
399	Child day care services	0	0	168	168
39	Maintenance and repair construction of nonresidential structures	0	60	102	162
325	Retail Stores - Health and personal care	0	2	159	161
391	Private elementary and secondary schools	0	0	160	160
377	Advertising and related services	0	86	73	160
387	Investigation and security services	0	82	74	156
393	Other private educational services	0	2	145	146
419	Personal care services	0	0	140	140
268	Switchgear and switchboard apparatus manufacturing	131	6	1	138
336	Transit and ground passenger transportation	0	61	67	128
323	Retail Stores - Building material and garden supply	0	3	124	127
427	US Postal Service	0	57	64	120
384	Office administrative services	0	78	41	119
409	Amusement parks, arcades, and gambling industries	0	0	114	114
339	Couriers and messengers	0	57	56	113
424	Grantmaking, giving, and social advocacy organizations	0	0	113	113
326	Retail Stores - Gasoline stations	0	1	111	112
340	Warehousing and storage	0	45	66	111
328	Retail Stores - Sporting goods, hobby, book and music	0	1	108	109
432	Other state and local government enterprises	0	13	92	106
407	Fitness and recreational sports centers	0	32	71	102
36	Construction of other new nonresidential structures	100	0	0	100
376	Scientific research and development services	0	61	39	99

Sector	Sector Description	Direct	Indirect	Induced	Total
401	Community food, housing, and other relief services, including rehabilitation services	0	0	96	96
403	Spectator sports companies	0	33	60	92
402	Performing arts companies	0	29	63	92
31	Electric power generation, transmission, and distribution	32	13	43	88
410	Other amusement and recreation industries	0	19	67	87
113	Printing	0	43	42	86
404	Promoters of performing arts and sports and agents for public figures	0	19	63	81
370	Specialized design services	0	69	12	81
322	Retail Stores - Electronics and appliances	0	1	76	77
338	Scenic and sightseeing transportation and support activities for transportation	0	32	45	77
20	Extraction of oil and natural gas	0	14	58	73
321	Retail Stores - Furniture and home furnishings	0	1	71	72
346	Motion picture and video industries	0	32	37	69
421	Dry-cleaning and laundry services	0	10	59	68
345	Software publishers	44	15	10	68
423	Religious organizations	0	0	65	65
238	Broadcast and wireless communications equipment manufacturing	57	4	1	61
422	Other personal services	0	5	56	61
332	Transport by air	0	22	39	61
2	Grain farming	0	4	57	61
359	Funds, trusts, and other financial vehicles	0	1	58	59
19	Support activities for agriculture and forestry	0	4	53	57
341	Newspaper publishers	0	24	32	56
352	Data processing, hosting, ISP, web search portals and related services	16	10	28	54
417	Commercial and industrial machinery and equipment repair and maintenance	0	25	28	53
TOTAL		12,039	5,516	15,235	32,790